Does Re
Do More
Harm Th
Good?

Booklets in the Searching Issues series:

Does Religion Do More Harm Than Good?

NICKY GUMBEL

Scripture quotations taken from
the Holy Bible, New International
Version Anglicised. Copyright ©
1979, 1984, 2011 Biblica, formerly
International Bible Society. Used by
permission of Hodder & Stoughton
Publishers, an Hachette UK
company. All rights reserved. 'NIV'
is a registered trademark of Biblica.
UK trademark number 1448790.

Published by Alpha International
HTB Brompton Road
London SW7 IJA
Email: publications@alpha.org
Website: alpha.org
@alphacourse

Illustrated by Charlie Mackesy

Contents

Does Religion Do More Harm Than Good?

At HTB church in London, we pray for various groups in the congregation who work in different sectors. I recall a time when we met to pray for those involved in British politics, government and public life. Among the group were four Members of Parliament, two senior police officers and many others working within the police, the Foreign Office and the Civil Service. Speaking with this group afterwards, it became evident that these Christians had concerns about their place in contemporary public life. A member of the Civil Service told of how his colleague, a man in a senior position, was an active member of the British Humanist Society. The colleague believes people of faith should be kept out of the Civil Service, since their views and decisions would be negatively affected by their beliefs. This man had recently been placed on the recruitment committee.

Many people experience similar antipathy towards faith in public life, whether at school or university, or in various professions. A number of people have said that in education, the judiciary and the medical profession – roles that comprise elements of influence, care or vulnerability – there are certain situations in which it has become extremely difficult to be a Christian today.

Tobias Jones, writing in *The Guardian*, said, 'Until a few years ago religion was similar to soft drugs: a blind eye was turned to private use, but woe betide you if you were caught dealing.'[1] That mood is changing. No longer is it assumed that the church is a good thing – a benefit to the society – whether or not others believe in the faith of that church. Perhaps for the first time since Constantine (AD 272–337), Christianity in the West is on the back foot.

"I've got an ounce of New testament if you're interested"

One of Richard Dawkins' documentaries about religion was entitled *The Root of All Evil*. In it, the prominent atheist suggests that, far from making people better or doing good things in society, 'faith is one of the world's great evils,' and he describes the God of the Bible as an 'evil monster'. He is not alone in this view. Peter Watson, author of a recent book on the history of invention, was asked by the *New York Times* to name humanity's worst invention. He answered, 'Without question, ethical monotheism... This has been responsible for most of the wars and bigotry in history.'[2] So, how do Christians respond to the charge that religion does more harm than good in society?

First, Christians should acknowledge that actions carried out in the name of Jesus have sometimes caused considerable harm. The Crusades of the Middle Ages and the European religious wars of the sixteenth century are just two examples of times when religious zeal has caused great harm to many people. But the harm caused by groups of Christians at some periods of history should not lead us to regard the entirety of Christianity as intrinsically harmful to society. Though these acts were carried out in the name of Christ, it is right to ask whether they were in line with the teachings of Christ himself. The answer is resolutely 'no'. Christ has taught his followers to turn the other cheek (Luke 6:29) and, when conflict broke out between his followers and those who opposed him, he stopped the fighting and even healed the wounded enemy (Luke 22:51). Their actions were not in keeping with those of Christ.

Leading scientist Francis Collins writes that, when it comes to 'the hypocritical behavior of those who profess belief... [we need to] keep in mind that the pure water of spiritual truth is carried in those rusty containers called human beings'.[3]

The God of the Bible

Today's critics of religion are not the first to suggest that the God of the Bible is an 'evil monster'. In 1795, Thomas Paine wrote in *Age of Reason*:

> Whenever we read... the cruel and tortuous executions, the unrelenting vindictiveness with which more than half the Bible is filled, it would be more consistent that we call it the word of a demon than the word of God. It is a history of wickedness that has served to corrupt and brutalise humankind and for my own part, I sincerely detest it, as I detest everything that is cruel.[4]

How do we respond to this? We might consider three points in brief.

Examine the evidence of the whole Bible

Critics of the Bible are extremely selective in the passages of the Bible upon which they base their description of God. Any reader of the Bible will struggle to comprehend how Israel's actions in attacking surrounding nations served the justice of God. And yet, these same parts of the Old Testament also maintain that God is incredibly merciful and compassionate. When Abraham intercedes with God on behalf of the nations (Genesis 18), he finds that God will pardon the wickedness of the city for the sake of just a few good men and women. Similarly, in the middle of the narrative recounting how God broke Israel free from the oppressive hand of the Egyptian nation, even though the focus is on the just punishment of human wickedness, Moses still finds time to declare the goodness of God:

> The Lord, the Lord, the compassionate and gracious God, slow to anger, abounding in love and faithfulness, maintaining love to thousands, and forgiving wickedness, rebellion and sin.
> Exodus 34:6–7

Likewise, the prophetic literature focuses on God as one who is supremely concerned about social justice and caring for the poor. Through Zechariah, for example, God says:

> This is what the Lord Almighty said: 'Administer true justice; show mercy and compassion to one another. Do not oppress the widow or the fatherless, the foreigner or the poor.'
> Zechariah 7:9–10

It will always be possible to cherry-pick extreme examples, taking them out of context in order to build up a horrible picture of God as an 'evil monster'. Nevertheless, the Bible demands to be read as a whole. It paints a picture of a loving and good God. While we struggle to understand how some of the events the Bible recounts fit within that picture of God, we should not let them obscure the rest.

I have endeavoured to read the whole Bible every year since I have been a Christian (over thirty-five years), and I simply do not recognise the God that Thomas Paine and the New Atheists describe. I certainly do not believe in the God they describe; the God I know is totally different. He is a God of love, whose love for us is as high as the heavens are above the earth, whose compassion is like that of a parent caring for his children. He is a God of justice and love, a God of kindness and compassion, and a God of mercy and grace (Psalm 103:11–13).

Read the Bible through the lens of Jesus

The Bible is meant to be read in the context of a living relationship with the God who is its central character. Reading the Bible is not an academic exercise but the expression of a relationship. Faith is about putting our trust in the God who speaks to us through his Word. God has revealed himself in the Bible. It is possible, as Jesus said, to hold to the Scriptures, but not read them in the context of this life-giving relationship: 'You diligently study the Scriptures because you think that by them you possess eternal life. These are the Scriptures that testify about me, yet you refuse to come to me to have life' (John 5:39).

As Christians, we believe that Jesus is the image of the invisible God; Jesus said, 'Anyone who has seen me has seen the Father' (John 14:9). In Luke 24:27, we read that 'beginning with Moses and all the Prophets, he [Jesus] explained to them what was said in all the Scriptures concerning himself'. By looking at the Scriptures through the lens of Jesus, the Old Testament turns into a Christian text. We have to look at the Old Testament through the life, character, death and resurrection of Jesus. For example, we might consider Jesus' death: Jesus did not do violence, but he allowed violence to be done to him; he gave his life as a ransom on our behalf. Many passages in the Old Testament change shape when considered in this way.

We also need to look at the Scriptures through the lens of Jesus' teaching. Jesus said, 'Do to others as you would have them do to you' (Luke 6:31); 'Love your neighbour as yourself' (Matthew 22:39); 'Love your enemies and pray for those who persecute you' (Matthew 5:44). Again, we should interpret the Old Testament through this lens.

Recognise the positive impact of the Bible

We should remember that Jesus' teaching is pivotal in the history of Western civilisation. It has provided a moral code: an absolute right and an absolute wrong; an absolute good and an absolute evil. If the God of the Bible is to be dismissed, the moral code will be turned on its head. Or it will need a new basis, if there can be one.

The Bible itself has formed the historic basis for society's understanding of what good and evil are. If that basis is to be done away with, and God written off as an 'evil monster', questions must be asked about what moral path society will follow. In this regard, what little those making the charge have to offer as alternatives is troubling to say the least. If we are just a product of our genes and our environment, or if we are dancing to the tune of our DNA,[5] then there is no place for absolute standards of morality, which become purely subjective. Rod Liddle wrote in the *Sunday Times*:

Nowhere though do atheists flail more ineffectually than in attempting to fill what Sartre called the 'God-shaped Hole' inside all of us: our need to believe in something from which we derive our notion of morality. Dawkins acknowledges this need for something and concocts 10 commandments. In place of don't kill, steal or covet your neighbour's wife, he has things like, 'Value the future on a timescale longer than your own', or, 'Enjoy your own sex life (so long as it damages nobody else).' It is the 10 Commandments handed down... not in stone but perhaps on organic tofu. It is beyond parody, and its potential longevity as a useful moral code can be counted in years rather than millenniums.[6]

When the absolute standard is removed, all that remains is utilitarianism; and utilitarian ethics have worrying implications. In the afterword to John Brockman's book *What is Your Dangerous Idea?* Dawkins wrote this on the subject of eugenics:

I wonder whether, some sixty years after Hitler's death, we might at least venture to ask what the moral difference is between breeding for musical ability and forcing a child to take music lessons. Or why it is acceptable to train

> fast runners and high jumpers and not to breed them... hasn't the time come when we should stop being frightened to ask the question?... It is harder than most people realise to justify the unique and exclusive status that *Homo sapiens* enjoys in our unconscious assumptions. Why does 'pro life' always mean 'pro human life?' Why are so many people outraged at the idea of killing an eight-celled human conceptus while cheerfully masticating a steak that cost the life of an adult, sentient, and probably terrified cow?[7]

Dawkins thus implies that there is no absolute reason to prefer people to cows. Hitchens too often refers to people as mammals. Yet if human beings are not distinguished from animals, the sanctity of human life is abandoned in favour of principles such as, 'It is wrong to reduce the amount of worthwhile life.'

Recently I saw an item on the news about Sister Frances Dominica, who won the Woman of the Year Award in 2007. Sister Frances started Helen House, which cares for very sick and dying children in Oxfordshire, England, providing practical and spiritual support for parents and families trying to look after such children at home. It is deeply moving to see Sister Frances and the people who work at Helen House caring for these children with life-threatening and terminal illnesses in the most loving way, giving them the best possible life for their very short period on this earth. It begs the question, 'Why do they do it?' They do it because they believe in the God of the Bible and in the sanctity of human life: that every child, however disabled, is made in the image of God and is loved by and precious to him. The God of the Bible as revealed in Jesus Christ is not an evil monster but the only hope for the future of our civilisation.

Is faith really 'one of the world's great evils'?

Faith has been described as 'one of the world's great evils, comparable to the smallpox virus but harder to eradicate'.[8] Let us consider three aspects of this belief.

Distinguish between faith and the misuse of faith

As we saw above, the Crusades represented a *misuse* of the Christian faith. It is imperative for both those of faith and none to distinguish between the use and misuse of their beliefs. The leading atheists focus only on the *misuse* of faith, never on its use for good. However, in contrast, when it comes to secular ideologies, they focus only on their use for good, never on misuse. Paul Copan writes:

> Much of the blood shed in the 20th century was the result of atheist ideologues. It's ironic that religion gets the blame for violence, but critics of religion are silent when a secular or atheistic faith – such as that of Stalin or Mao Tse-tung – wreaks utter destruction on millions upon millions of lives.[9]

Even the advances of modern science can be abused, as the development of napalm, landmines and gas chambers shows. In the same way, faith can be abused through its *misuse*. As Canon David Watson often used to say, 'The opposite of misuse is not disuse, it is right use.' This is a reflection echoed by the Northern Irish Christian writer John Lennox, who has experienced at first hand the harm religious conflict and the misuse of faith can bring:

As a Northern Irishman, I am all too familiar with a certain brand of sectarian violence where a religious history has been used to fan the flames of terrorism (on both sides of the divide); although, as historians point out, a whole additional complex of political and social factors has been at work that makes analysis in terms of religion alone far too simplistic. What, then, have I to say about this evil aspect of religion?

The first thing to say is that I roundly condemn and abhor it, every bit as much as the New Atheists. I do so, be it noted, as a Christian. For, although the New Atheists' charge against Christendom for its violence may well be justified, their charge is not valid against the teaching of Christ himself... People who engage in violent and cruel activities at any time, in Northern Ireland or the Balkans or anywhere else, while invoking the name of God, are certainly *not* obeying Christ when they do so, whatever they may say to the contrary. After all, the name 'Christian' means a disciple or follower of Jesus Christ. Following Christ means obeying his commandments. And one of those commands was the explicit *prohibition* of the use of force to defend Christ or his message... So let it be said loudly and clearly – it will have to be loud to be heard above the caterwauling of the New Atheists – *Christ repudiated violence*. He would not allow force to be used to save him from false accusation, suffering, and even death.[10]

Remember the harm done in the name of atheism

The premise of the New Atheism is that the world would be vastly improved if only we could get rid of religion. The acclaimed journalist John Humphrys writes that 'for atheists to claim that without religion peace and harmony would reign is patently absurd. It's not the Bible that proves that. It's the history books.'[11] Keith Ward, formerly of Oxford University, points out what we saw above – that, 'The two world wars were not fought on religious grounds at all... there were no religious doctrines or practices at issue in those wars. The most terrible conflicts in human history were not religious.'[12]

Evil things *have* been done in the name of atheism. Humphrys reminds us that this includes terrorism itself – despite its frequent association with religion. The British political philosopher John Gray makes the point that, 'It is easy to forget how during the twentieth century terror was used on a vast scale by secular regimes... "The roots of contemporary terrorism are in radical Western ideology – especially Leninism – far more than in religion".'[13] It is estimated that, in the USSR, 20 million were killed; in China: 65 million; in North Korea: 2 million and in Cambodia: 2 million.

At least some of this terrorism was carried out by atheistic regimes *against* people of faith and religion itself. It is estimated that the total number of people killed by Communist governments through the extermination of their own population and carrying out explicitly antireligious policies is somewhere between 85 and 100 million. John Cornwell, Fellow of Jesus College, Cambridge, points out that, 'Stalin's atheism, moreover, was a crucial feature of his entire ideology. He oppressed, imprisoned, murdered [Christians], destroying their... churches throughout the length and breadth of Russia.'[14] In a speech given on 18 November 1961, Krushchev, who led the Soviet Union at that time, outlined their philosophy, saying, 'We need a considered and well balanced system of scientific atheistic education which would embrace all strata and groups of the population and prevent the spread of religious views especially among children and adolescents.'[15]

Both Christianity and atheism have at times brought harm to our world. But harm comes about through *misuse*. Nobody is suggesting that all atheists do terrible things. My father was an atheist (or, at least, an agnostic), and he was a wonderful man, one of the heroes of my life.

Appreciate the good done in the name of Jesus

While Christians have done harm in history, it is not true that the church has consistently done more harm than good. Author and theologian Jonathan Hill acknowledges that much that has been done in the name of Christianity has been bad but warns us to acknowledge that this does not define Christianity as a whole:

> The Christian churches, like any other social institution, have a very complex history and make-up. Clearly, they've not been simply shining beacons of goodness, and I wouldn't wish to pretend that they have. But by the same token, they've not been simply terrible sources of evil...[16]

Unfortunately, the critics of Christianity fixate so much upon the bad that they do not see that the church has always strived imperfectly to be a source of blessing. One example is the remarkable achievement of Christians in establishing hospitals throughout Europe. The Christians of the Middle Ages were unique in establishing leper colonies, caring for those whom other societies 'banished from all human habitations'. Christians have been establishing hospitals and centres of care since the days of the Roman empire. There was no precedent for this act of love and care in the pagan society out of which it emerged.

When the plague hit the Greek city of Edessa, St Ephraim (AD 306–73) established a hospital there to care for the afflicted. St Basil the Great (AD 329–79) established a leper colony in Cappadocia. In Constantinople, rich members of the laity served the poor, bathed the sick and gave alms for centuries. Indeed, these acts of charity were never more extensive than in the Middle Ages themselves, when the Crusades also took place. During this time the Benedictine monks alone were responsible for 2,000 hospitals in Western Europe. Such centres fed the hungry, cared for widows and orphans and distributed alms. Increasingly, these centres of medical care also became centres of training, and so provided the forerunner to today's network of medical care and training.

Christianity, it must therefore be said, has also done a great deal of good in society. Theologian and philosopher David Bentley Hart suggests that, more often, historians looking closely at the Middle Ages with all the horrors of the Crusades see 'a society that, for all its brutalities, mixed motives and inconstancies, was in some genuine way constructed around a central ideal of Christian love.'[17]

Over the centuries, millions of ordinary Christians around the world have done good. Even people who are not Christians themselves recognise the good that is being done in the name of Jesus. John Humphrys is an agnostic and describes himself as a 'failed atheist'. After his programme on Radio 4 *In Search of God* he received hundreds of letters in response to his search.

He writes:

> For every sceptic, there were dozens of believers who said they had been converted by a specific event or experience... They are overwhelmingly sincere people who, one way or another, had found belief in God and that belief has changed their lives... most of the writers strike me as intelligent, discriminating people who have given a lot of thought to their faith, asked a lot of questions and usually managed to satisfy their doubts... . For every fanatic there are countless ordinary, decent people who believe in... God and wish no harm to anyone. Many of them regard it as their duty to try to make the world a better place.[18]

In a radio interview some time before his death, author and prominent atheist Christopher Hitchens said, 'There is nothing that someone of faith can do that someone without can't do; there are no benefits that a Christian can make to society that a secular person can't also achieve.' After listening to the radio programme, Charlie Mackesy, the artist and sculptor, wrote down the response that he would have given, had he been at the interview:

> All I can say, and I can only speak for myself, Christopher, is that there are things with faith in Jesus that I've done that I'd never have had the courage to do, ever; never had the patience to do; never had the love and the freedom to do; never had the inspiration or the guts to do; and never had the desire to do. I'm sure others without faith could achieve more, much more, but for me, without it, I would never have tried or attempted and failed, sometimes half of it. Jesus brings life and guts and courage into everything, for me.[19]

Christians do not claim to be better than those who are not; simply better than who they would have been, had they not become Christians. The gospel, the good news of Jesus, brings freedom and liberation to our lives, and the Holy Spirit transforms us from within. 'The fruit of the Spirit is love, joy, peace, patience, kindness, goodness, faithfulness, gentleness and self-control' (Galatians 5:22–23). We see this fruit in the lives of people who follow Jesus, in their desire to care for the poor, visit the prisons, and care for the dying. Can it really be said that religion is one of the world's great evils?

Conclusion

I used to be an atheist with very similar views, though they were, of course, not as developed as those of the New Atheists. Then I encountered Jesus Christ and discovered a relationship with him: a relationship with the God of the Bible who is not an evil monster. I experienced God's amazing love poured into my heart by the Holy Spirit, which gave me a love for God and a love for other people. That was one of the experiences that led me to become a vicar, because I long for other people to experience that same love in their own lives. Over the years I have seen the impact of this faith on our marriage and family life, and I have seen the impact of Christian faith on other families in our church. I have watched its impact on the young children, the teenagers, the students and young adults who have grown up in a community of faith.

I have also watched people coming to faith in Jesus on Alpha at HTB, and I have heard many more stories from all around the world. They tell of changed lives: people whose marriages have been restored, whose relationships with their parents or children have changed beyond recognition, people who have been set free from addiction, or who were in prison and have come to faith in Jesus. They speak about how their faith has changed them, and how they are now making a contribution to society. Some have started ministries caring for the poor, for the homeless, and for people with AIDS. Why? Because they have experienced faith in Jesus Christ.

The small things that individual people do – acts of forgiveness, acts of love, acts of service – can be multiplied to millions and millions; they happen every day and are not necessarily recorded or known about, other than by very few. I cannot speak for religion in general, but I can tell you because I have seen it with my own eyes, that faith in Jesus Christ does not do harm – it does an immeasurable amount of good – because we follow the one who 'went around doing good' (Acts 10:38).

Endnotes

1. Tobias Jones, 'Secular fundamentalists are the new totalitarians', *The Guardian*, 6 January 2007.

2. *New York Times*, 11 December 2005, nytimes.com/2005/12/11/magazine/11wwln_q4.html?_r=0

3. Francis Collins, *The Language of God* (Simon & Schuster, 2007), p.231.

4. Thomas Paine, *Age of Reason* (1795), quoted in Brian McLaren, *Everything Must Change* (Nelson Books, 2008), p.157.

5. Dawkins writes that, 'DNA neither cares nor knows. DNA just is. And we dance to its music.' In Richard Dawkins, *River Out of Eden: A Darwinian View of Life* (Phoenix, 1996), p.155.

6. Rod Liddle, *Sunday Times*, 8 October 2006.

7. John Brockman, *What is Your Dangerous Idea? Today's Leading Thinkers on the Unthinkable* (Simon & Schuster, 2006), p.300.

8. Christopher Hitchens, *Letters to a Young Contrarian* (Basic Books, 2005), p.55.

9. Paul Copan, 'Jesus, Religions and Just War' (Ravi Zacharias International Ministries USA, 2007) http://www.everystudent.com/wires/justwar.html

10. John Lennox, *Gunning for God: A Critique of the New Atheism* (Lion, 2011), pp.64–65.

11. John Humphrys, *In God We Doubt* (Hodder, 2008), p.184.

12. Keith Ward, *Is Religion Dangerous?* (Lion, 2006), p.74.

13. John Humphrys, *op cit.*, p.293.

14. John Cornwell, *Darwin's Angel* (Profile Books, 2008), p.90.

15. Michael Bourdeaux, *Patriarch and Prophets: Persecution of the Russian Orthodox Church* (Mowbrays, 1975), p.38.

16. 'Christianity's Cultural Contributions: Rob Moll interviews Jonathan Hill', *Christianity Today*, March 2006.

17. David Bentley Hart, *Atheist Delusions: The Christian Revolution and Its Fashionable Enemies* (Yale University Press, 2009), p.31.

18. John Humphrys, *op cit*, pp.217, 232, 322.
19. Charlie Mackesy, from a talk given at HTB, London, 6 January 2008.

Alpha

Alpha is a practical introduction to the Christian faith, initiated by HTB in London and now being run by thousands of churches, of many denominations, throughout the world. If you are interested in finding out more about the Christian faith and would like details of your nearest Alpha, please visit our website:

alpha.org

or contact:
The Alpha Office,
HTB Brompton Road,
London,
SW7 1JA

Tel: 0845 644 7544

About the Author

Nicky Gumbel is the pioneer of Alpha. He read law at Cambridge and theology at Oxford, practised as a barrister and is now vicar of HTB in London. He is the author of many bestselling books about the Christian faith, including *Questions of Life*, *The Jesus Lifestyle*, *Why Jesus?*, *A Life Worth Living*, *Searching Issues* and *30 Days*.

CPSIA information can be obtained
at www.ICGtesting.com
Printed in the USA
LVHW040305031118
595815LV00006B/30/P